# ROADWAYS AND STARDUST

# TO
# SHEILA

# ROADWAYS
### AND
# STARDUST

BY

## PAUL J. PEASE

WITH FOREWORD BY
### BEATRICE CHASE

JAMIESON & MUNRO, LTD.
STIRLING

PUBLISHED    -    1934

*Printed in Great Britain*
*at the Observer Press, Stirling.*

# CONTENTS.

# FOREWORD

THE typescript of " Roadways and Stardust " reached me one April day and I settled down to read it, in the Room of Sunshine.

It was a typical April day. A strong, warm southerly wind was shaking the casement with impatient fingers, while her rustling robes brushed over the dancing golden daffodils and shook the cascades of violet aubretia in the grey old beds outside the window. Inside, a merry fire prattled to itself, and Tiger Puss, who is thirteen this month, reposed on a velvet cushion at my feet. I opened the typescript and was quickly transported to a Land of Mystic Romance—a land which, alas, I have never yet seen. " Absurd ! " some reader may exclaim. " How can anyone who has never seen Scotland write a preface to a Scottish book ? "

If I may venture a reply, this makes the book's charm more conclusive than if I knew the Highlands. If the word painting has the power so to transport me, so to show me, by mental imagery, this unknown land, what will its effect be on those who know and love each name in it ? The effect will be incalculable.

The book has made me love the Highlands, their people and their animals, their mountains, lochs and mists. To those who already love all these, it will be like a draught of rare wine.

To stress one feature of the work, the author has a special genius for the Night. His descriptions of

sunset, twilight, early dawn, besides the mysteries
of deep night are haunting.

Constantly, too, one comes upon words of cheer
rendered the more telling of their natural analogy.
On the very first page, in " Highland Blue," we find
this beautiful comparison concerning the Clyde ferry.

" In the morning, I, too, shall join the throng
and be floated across the Styx. But there will be
no Cerberus guarding the far side. Half way
across, I shall give a few pennies to Charon, and
then when we touch land, I shall have forgotten
the drabness, the rain and the mental and spiritual
poverty I left behind. Surely, life treats us in
the same way as the ferry serves our needs. We are
floated across our difficulties."

A little further on, we come to the Pass of
Brander.

" The Pass of Brander is forbidding enough to
pander to the most morbid desire for oppression.
Were I a poet, I should symbolise those bare,
unforgiving cliffs, which rise so sheer from the
dark waters of Loch Awe, as the narrow way which
we must tread alone to that fuller life which awaits
us at the End of the Road."

There is nothing so consoling in the spiritual
life as such comparisons from Nature. The inspired
words of the Shepherd King ring on immortal down
the ages : " I have lifted up mine eyes to the mountains from whence cometh my help," and Mr. Pease,
in a true and witty passage, describes the discussion
of troubles at the foot of a mountain and how these
same troubles are forgotten by the wanderer's return
to the same spot.

Every hill lover will shake hands with him for this alone. How many times have I mounted to a Dartmoor Tor and exclaimed " Now I don't care what happens ! "

There is some strange, mysterious and infallible strength and healing in mountain country—even in the mere reading about mountain country.

Animals of all sorts drift across his pages. The story of the fiery corn-eating monster which resolves itself into a bull swimming the strait by moonlight and emerging from the water sparkling with phosphorescence, is most impressive and perfectly possible. The reverse of the coin is the tragic story of the ill-treated horse which first made our author realise his kinship with animals.

One feature of the book which has aroused my warmest sympathy is the descriptions of the portable wireless.

Among a certain section of the public, the wireless is supposed to desecrate lonely places, I myself used to think so—till I was given a set of my own. Of course, some radio performances would jar, but what could be more appropriate to a camp of lively young folk, than a perfectly-played dance orchestral programme ?

Again, the description of hearing the nightingale on the Clyde, relayed from Berkshire, is one of the most beautiful pieces of lyrical writing in the book.

And how can anyone say that the solemn voice of our beloved Big Ben tolling midnight in the hills is out of place ? Is an old friend anywhere out of place ? And is not the death and birth of a new day heard in perfect setting as at the camp fire scene near Crieff?

Again, what more fitting setting could there be for the beautiful Thursday night service by Canon Elliot, than the waters of the loch surrounded by mountains, while the fishers lay on their oars in their skiffs to listen? I do not remember ever having read any treatise about the miracle of wireless which has so appealed to me as the scattered idylls about it from the Highlands described in this little book.

The sympathy with nature, with animals, with humanity, the lessons taught by all, the comradeship of the open road, which leads nearer to the stars, are all here—and, fittingly, partly because of its title, partly because heaven with its myriad stars is our goal, the book ends with the stars.

BEATRICE CHASE.

# HIGHLAND BLUE.

IT is night, and yet the ferry ploughs tirelessly across the Clyde. I lie in my tent and observe its ceaseless journeyings. Beyond Old Kilpatrick are the hills I love so well, but the road to them is made possible only by this ungainly Ferry—this snorting, clanking, river rider.

In the morning I, too, shall join the throng and be floated across the Styx. But there will be no Cerberus guarding the far side. Half way across I shall give a few pennies to Charon, and then when we touch land, I shall have forgotten the drabness, the rain and the mental and spiritual poverty I left behind.

Surely life treats us in the same way as the ferry serves our needs. We are floated across our difficulties.

With the coming of a new day, I take the road which winds about Loch Lomondside. The great peace of a Highland Sabbath lies over the land, and the blue waters have a fascination all their own. On the steep bank the woods are carpeted with wild hyacinths, and the " wee birdies " chant their rhapsody of spring.

Suddenly, I come across a mysterious sign bearing the inscription " S.Y.H.A." Not altogether without risk of accident, I turned the car off the road until a burn prevents me taking it any further. There is a rough bridge across the burn, and crossing it, I see in front of me the Inverbeg Hostel of the Scottish Youth Hostels Association.

To the right of the hut are little groups of boys and girls sun-bathing. Going into the " common room " I meet a young man, simply, but appropriately attired in an abbreviated pair of shorts. He has been explaining to a girl the essential points of a new collapsible cooker.

The warden then takes my membership card, and hands out stores. He tells me a story or two, shows me every detail of the place (in which I am profoundly interested) so that in a very short space of time I am able to appreciate the jolly paganism of a Youth Hostel.

In the hillside behind the hut is a rocky pool, fed by an icy mountain burn. Two ardent spirits prevail upon me to bathe. " Not so bad if you're used to it." I agree, as we towel vigorously in the warm sunshine. In the evening everybody sits round the common room and sings. But it is a moonlight night, and under the witchery of this spell, some of the members decide to climb Ben Lomond to see the sun rise.

For myself, I find the straw palliasses, which the Hostel provides, extremely comfortable. Therefore, I wake up thoroughly refreshed and ready for the road again.

The Highroad to Heaven is notoriously a difficult one. Certainly the road between Crianlarich and Dalmally must prove to some of us more timorous beings a region of desolation. The Pass of Brander is forbidding enough to pander to the most morbid desire for oppression. Were I a poet I should symbolize those bare, unforgiving cliffs, which rise so sheer from the dark waters of Loch Awe, as the narrow way which we must tread alone to that fuller life which awaits us at the End of the Road.

For this reason alone, perhaps, I shall ever hold dear the memory of arriving at Connel—Connel with its cream and white houses which bask on the shores of Loch Etive, and Connel with its bridge spanning the Loch at the Falls of Lora. It is said that the girders of the bridge set up a great song when the wind blows fresh and strong from the sea.

I am also informed that the " Dunstaffnage Arms Hotel " is the oldest building in Connel. The " Dunstaffnage Arms " is undoubtedly one of those Inns where a man might wisely choose to spend a honeymoon. There are occasions, I think, when luxury and quaintness should replace vagabondage and romance. Therefore, I abandon my idea of camping, yielding myself unreservedly to the unquestioned delights of a feather bed, to the artistic rapture of embroidered sheets. Against my better judgment I surrender the claims of the straw palliasse to the caress of the perfect bed !

The sun sets in a haze of glory over Lismore, and at night, while I sit writing at an uncurtained window, I can still see away over the waters of Loch Etive to the mountains of Appin. I pay homage to the joy of setting foot within the Kingdom of Argyll.

From Connel there are two ways by which the traveller may reach Kinlochleven. The first is by crossing the Connel Ferry Railway Viaduct, and thus straight to Ballachulish ; the second by the Pass of Glencoe.

B

Choosing the latter and by far the longer route, I come first to Tyndrum from whence the road ascends until the Perthshire-Argyll boundary is reached at a height of 1033 feet. I am on the Great Western Highway—the new road, which must be among the greatest works of engineering ever achieved in Britain. I was never privileged to traverse the Glen before the coming of the new road (for I sympathise with those who think that the Glen should have been left untouched by the hand of progress). Yet in imagination I see something in the new road of man's most valiant fight with adverse conditions of climate, rock and bogland. I see something in the new road of man's eternal struggle to do better than he did before—man's effort to see where he went wrong, and man's enthusiasm to start again and win through.

Ben Odhar is hiding his head among the clouds, and everywhere rainstorms are gathering . . . . " The Glen o' Weeping " is in tears to-day. At Bridge of Orchy, the new road diverts the original course of this journey to the east side of Loch Tulla, for it is here, at the time of writing, that the road has yet to be " surfaced." My speed is reduced, and I lumber along towards the Kingshouse where the road is once more complete.

Down by Loch Tulla is the dwelling of the road constructors. It is a little group of tin huts completely isolated from the world of affairs, in a setting of superb Highland loveliness. Not one motorist in a hundred would have thought of stopping to enter the cookhouse, which is the excuse I offer for so doing.

Two men are peeling potatoes, and I learn from them that there are forty labourers still engaged on this section of the roadway. Men have been working on the new road over a period of five years.

There is art in the building of fine bridges, for I cross more than one which arrests the attention of the most casual.

As I come to the mouth of the gorge, that pass, in which there happened that most foul massacre, when guest set upon host, and Highland hospitality was villainously outraged, the mist of rain envelopes the mountains, and there is no sound in all that desolation, but the rush of the torrents as they hurl themselves from the heights above.

I am fairly set in the midst of the pass, when I am brought to a halt by the petrol tank running dry. Just as the car slackens to a halt, a wayfarer heaves up out of the mist ; and I offer him the shelter of the car. He, too, is making for Kinlochleven, so I gladly seize the opportunity of taking him there, and thus secure company on the lone road. While we sit waiting for the rain to clear sufficiently to allow of the tank being filled from the spare, I expect this rain-drenched Highlander to speak of the Massacre of 1692, when thirty-eight Macdonalds of Glencoe were murdered in their beds by the Campbells of Glenlyon. Instead he tells me of the coming of the Highroad from Glencoe along Loch Levenside by Kinlochleven to North Ballachulish.

I am informed that before the Great War there was only a footpath to take the traveller from South Ballachulish to Kinlochleven, and not a very good footpath at that. Indeed, the only sensible approach to Kinlochleven was by steamer up the Loch. German prisoners were, however, detailed to blast

the hillside for the highway which now allows of easy
access to the outpost of industry represented by the
Kinlochleven aluminium works.

My companion recalls a wild winter's night some
twenty years ago. He was then but a lad, and had
made a long journey alone, arriving at South Ballachulish after the sailing of the last steamer, which
would have taken him to his home at Kinlochleven.
For some reason or other he was apparently too shy
to take up a lodging at Ballachulish, and so in the
teeth of the snow he made his way along the tortuous
path to where the lights of his home-town would
welcome him. He gained the threshold of the cottage
at one in the morning, and was well reprimanded for a
fool-hardy enterprise.

At length the rain abates, we fill the petrol tank
and pursue the journey through the Pass. On the
road stand four stags who scamper away at the
approach of the car, only to stand at a respectful
distance gazing curiously. I stop the car more
closely to observe their grace of movement, but they
do not seem to resent my presence. What shocking
condition they are in after the rigours of the winter !
My deep regret is that I did not bring any turnips
with me just in case I should encounter these divinities
of the high hills.

And so the new roads are bringing motorists to
the savage places—to the Glens and wild moorlands
which are the natural heritage of stags. Surely they
have a right to censure man for forcing his way thither.
My heart goes out to these noble creatures. I love
them.

Thus once more I have come to journey's end—

to Kinlochleven, which is one of the most remote towns in Scotland. It is a clear evening, and the waters of Loch Leven hold reflections of infinite beauty. If you throw a stone into the water, the mirror is broken, just as any action against nature blots out our vision of God. Man is like the Loch in that he can reflect all that which is beautiful only so long as he does not mar the peace which was intended for him.

Kinlochleven, which concerns the book " The Children of the Dead End," holds at once the romance of industry, and the romance of Highland Blue.

On approaching Kinlochleven one sees that the road (which runs high above the Loch) appears to end in the industrial town—seeming as much out of place in its Highland setting, as would a fish and chip saloon in a Cathedral Close. . . . But those who come here must look beyond the council houses, the electric lighting and the tennis courts, or try and accept this mushroom civilisation as contrast to the loveliness that is everywhere. A railway line connects the aluminium works with the pier on the Loch.

I am a guest to-night for my camp is in a hillside garden. The garden has an arbour set aside for quiet meditation ; but now the friendship of those who daily delight in this arbour, makes meditation give place to voiced emotions, mere words endeavouring, and in part succeeding, to tell of things most dear to us. Loneliness we have forgotten, and it is then that peace holds out her promise to us, for in these brief hours we share a common interest, and lay our twin ideals before the Highest Throne.

It is the setting time of the evening star.  We watch it as it dips down behind the purple mountains. Industry is asleep, Highland Blue has turned to night. We seek peace, and find it in the setting of a star.

## TOWARDS HUMANITY.

ON my way to Oban, I pitch camp on the shores of Benderloch by Ledaig. Around me in picturesque disorder is an upturned boat, a barrel and a rusty chain. I have my portable wireless with me, although a canny Highlander (who now perforce has to listen continually to the street music of electric cars), has informed me that music of this order in the Highlands would tend to desecration.

Personally, I approve of music on the Highroad. There are times, perhaps when the gnats are plaguing, and one has perforce to draw the tent flaps tightly to gain a little respite from the torture of them, when one is alone and hopelessly bounded by canvas walls, that the wireless comes into its own.

I do not brood upon the future, and speculate as to its possessions. I know only that I have a little lighted tent down by the seashore, and that it is filled with the song of great masters. But, nevertheless, my ears do not lose the music of the waters as they lap against the shore, nor the cry of the seabirds. I am alone, and yet the half of Europe is mine for entertainment.

To-day I have come down the coast near Oban and I am staying in a cottage by Loch Linnhe in the lands of Lorne. I am in bed (the guest chamber please, none of your camping this time) and by my side there is a glass of hot toddy. There is lemon in

it, and it is very sweet.    A Macdonald tartan spread
on the little table attracts me, and I am set wondering
once more how the Campbells could have gone through
with the Massacre of Glencoe.       Yes, it is all
very strange.   It was not very long ago that I was
in the house of a Campbell.    The Campbells gathered
round in the evening and sang Gaelic songs.    There
were nine Campbells and, with the obvious exception
of the girl at the piano, they all tried to sit on one sofa,
but the music they gave me was unforgettable in its
pagan directness.

The toddy is beginning to take effect ; my eyelids
are heavy, and I am deliciously comfortable.    When
I bathed to-night the water was tinged with a solution
of seaweed.    I stretch out my hand to snuff the candle,
and so very peacefully I fall asleep.

Highland hospitality has to be experienced to be
believed.   In the Highlands no door is ever shut to
him who may need food, shelter, and the good cheer
of honest company.   Your Scottish host has the true
art of friendliness.   For instance, he or more pointedly
she, does not govern her actions by what so and so
thinks, she merely does what is right and kind, and
suffers any man for whatever charm he may possess.

And, of course, the animals are welcome too.
Yesterday my hostess rescued a newly-born lamb
which had strayed from its mother and fallen over a
little cliff.   She brought it into the kitchen and laid
it in a basket before the fire—and the baby thing had
revived by the time she had sent for the farmer.

Need I say that the dogs, which are the unending
joy of the household, have thoroughly entered in to
the spirit of things ?   Three of them sleep in their

mistress's bedroom—two pugs and a Highland collie. The other night the pugs upset the basket which they share, and so the collie turned out of her basket, spending the remainder of the night on the floor, so that the disconsolate wanderings of the pugs might not disturb her beloved mistress.

In such surroundings it becomes increasingly difficult to " worry." But by the middle-day post I really had a great deal to " worry " about, so now that the evening has come we just leave all the wretched letters, dash out, and turn inland to the foot of a mountain. Here we solemnly enumerate our " worries "—thus number one, two, three and four. Then, with the dogs for company we start the ascent, but before very long the pugs are out of breath and have to be carried.

The summit gained we seek respite, and turn wondering eyes to the vision of splendid beauty that commands silence for its full appreciation—the sun is setting over the Sound of Mull and there are signs of a moon over Ben Cruachan.

When we have had our fill we dash down helter skelter, and so all out of breath and flushed with pleasure we arrive at the very spot where we first counted the " worries."

" Let me see, what were they ? " I ask.

" You may well ask," the girl returns, " we have left those worries at the top of the mountain—they simply do not exist."

The hill is called Cnoc Carna, but we have re-named it simply " Holy Mountain."

.    .    .    .    .    .

We have been having high jinks over the week-end trying to make peace with the pet sheep, who have very recently surrendered their winter coats to the shearer. These two sheep—mother and daughter—rejoicing in the new-found freedom of nudity, scamper hither and thither over the meadow, but seem always ready to respond to their mistress when she calls. She never forgets some special delicacy which they nibble gratefully from her hand.

But the mother sheep is still a trifle shy, having suffered the shearer many times previously.

Down by the seashore the other day I actually met that Mr. X. who confessed that his fear of suffering pain was a more potent force than his dislike of causing it ! He thought it was " so sentimental " not to have those sheep killed when they were worth good money at the butchers. He said that of course he wouldn't go near a slaughter yard " for anything," and that indeed it was really best for him not to think about slaughter at all, especially when he was enjoying his dinner.

We had been on the beach some time, when I noticed him raise a *whelk* to his mouth and eat it. Certainly some people are *not* particular as to their means of sustenance.

.  .  .  .  .  .

There is something about Oban that makes the stranger feel like a prodigal who has at last returned to his rightful home. When the battleships lie in the bay, out on their " exercises " from Southampton, you run into groups of English sailors on the front, whose speech contrasts so vividly with that of the holiday-makers from Glasgow . . . . One welcomes both for their own sakes.

The " front," too, is not just an aimless promenade, because there is always the interest of the bay with its varying craft. And then when you are past the residential houses with their gardens, you come to Dunollie Castle, looking, for all its hoary age, not at all forbidding, like some of the other Castles.

There have been several reasons why I have been very anxious to have an anti-vivisection meeting in its streets. We arranged last night that all the dogs at the cottage should attend our meeting, but we never really thought that they could make the affair the unexpected success they did.

Here they are! Two of them start a polite argument at just that crucial moment when the speaker is wondering if he is going to get an audience. Then the argument is joined by other dogs, and as it increases in volume and intensity a crowd begins to collect. It is so much easier to attract a crowd by letting them suppose a dog-fight to be in progress, than by giving them to understand that they are about to listen to an address which (for all they know) may not gain their interest, much less their sympathy.

The men who have been propping up the railing round the harbour wall, saunter across to see what it is all about. A policeman, prepared to interfere, approaches, but seeing that the dogs are merely members of the audience, decides that he need only remain " present " to quell any unseemly disturbance! Visitors join us, sailors join us, the dogs give up their argument as a bad job, and as though to crown our achievement Mr. X. (who doesn't care who vivisects who, so long as no one vivisects him) makes his way to the forefront of the gathering.

I become a central figure, I speak, and so my responsibility is fulfilled. But it was the dogs who had delivered us from the ignominy of delivering our meeting to a parked motor car and a passing message boy. And I noticed that Mr. X. never raised any objections to anything that was said at the meeting, although I naturally gave him every opportunity of doing so.

Dogs play such a prominent part in contemporary writings that I feel it would be imprudent to add here any discussion regarding their power of thought, devotion and heroism. Nevertheless I cannot leave this topic without mentioning a young Airedale who camped with me for a month last year, while I was by way of finding him a " good home." (Of course, I was not long in deciding that there was only one home in all the world and that was my own). " Jack "—I called my dog " Jack " because once an Irish Terrier of that name made good his escape from an Edinburgh Vivisection Laboratory—and I soon became the inseparable friends which Providence must have arranged that we should be.

Together with another Airedale he had previously been in the possession of a farmer who had conceived in his distorted mind the insane abomination of being brutal to them. Someone had investigated the whole sordid business, and the case had been duly tried before the Sheriff Court.

The dogs had been kept all day in a coal cellar. Although I have no record of what had been done to his mate, or of her subsequent fate after the summons, I do know that Jack had been throttled, stoned, repeatedly thrashed, and had had his head beaten on the ground. On one occasion Jack entered a neighbour's house, and the farmer came after him with a big leather whip and thrashed him . . . and for these crimes the Sheriff Court fined the farmer £3, with the option of twenty days' imprisonment, and further they admonished him for breach of the peace.

However, from the very first day when Jack first joined me and, sitting beside me in the car, gratefully licked my face for taking him, he looked to me for that sympathetic companionship which he needed so greatly. He would sleep on my bed, and accompany me to the bath, or when I went swimming. And because of these small privileges he at once assumed the duties of guarding me from known and unknown dangers. The terrors of the night had then but little significance.

I will not pretend that Jack always conducted himself in a saintly manner while we were in camp together. Indeed at times he behaved like an absolute heathen, as when he picked up some unsavoury intestines in a farm bothy, and was sick with rabbit's liver all over the running board of the car. He knew that this was a quite out of order procedure, so I did not have to mention the matter to him.

Sometimes Jack and I were obliged to eat at an hotel. We found certain hotel proprietors who declined to have a dog in their dining-rooms at any price. So it was that Jack and I took our food in the chauffeur's quarters, and I found that the chauffeurs appreciated my dog much better than those who used the dining-room, and who might, for convenience sake, leave their dogs (if they had any with them) elsewhere and in the charge of strangers.

Non-human fellow-creatures should be the especial concern of everyone, and we shall not have achieved progress in our time until they are.

## WITH INCIDENTAL MUSIC.

I HAVE pitched my tent to face the moonrise. I have left the inland Fjords, and I am trying to understand the mystery of Loch Awe. The tent is on a grass patch ringed by lupins, and straight down below lies the Loch. The moon has risen over the Bens, casting a gleaming road across the water ; the air is burdened with the cloying scent of herbs. If I really believed in fairies, I should expect to see them on such a night as this.

I return thanks for the voiceless wonder of this night on Loch Awe because it is so much better, I think, to be grateful for the calm while it lasts, than to cringe and pray for deliverance from the storm when it comes.

I recall sleeping out on the Fintry Moor above Kippen in Stirlingshire and having to endure the most dramatic storm of recent experience. At eleven thirty, after listening in to the evening programmes from London, I noticed the first flicker of lightning over the distant mountains. Gradually, as the onslaught advanced, the ground beneath me seemed to shake with the violence of the thunder and, protected only by the sparse covering of a tent, I was as though enveloped in a sheet of living flame.

To be plunged in inky darkness one moment, to see a familiar landscape in blinding light the next ; to be inactive in the midst of the fiercest battle is surely the most humiliating experience common to all vagabonds.

The Psalms of David contain some glorious references to storm. But while many can obtain æsthetic satisfaction in singing these Psalms, especially in a church where the organist is alive to the possibilities of his instrument, how few would find that same satisfaction lying out on the bare ground watching the storm grow nearer, listening to it overhead, and wondering if it will ever cease.

It is, as I said, a humbling experience, if it only causes one to realize man's impotence before the mighty voice of God.

The Fintry storm died away slowly even as it had begun, and at four in the morning came the calm of a gracious dawn.

And now since I have started looking back at " other days " let me introduce you to Peter who is one of the great unemployed. He introduces himself by saying that if I care to sleep on the floor of his tent I am a welcome visitor.

There have been some silly regulations as to where one may pitch camp, and I regretfully acknowledge defeat. Moreover, although not ordinarily concerned with inns or recommended hotels, it has been irritating to find that the inn has no sleeping accommodation. I am just facing up to the unpleasing prospects of sleeping in the car by the roadside, when I am accosted by this young fellow who makes a home of a tent at a permanent camp site.

Incidentally, I do not consider permanent camp sites in any way idealistic, but in my plight I gladly take advantage of the frank hospitality that is offered me. Possibly the best purpose served by permanent camps is giving the unemployed man something to do. They give him a " home " interest. Quite a lot of fellows who suffer unemployment avoid the City, only going there once a week to draw the dole, or to " sign the bureau."

After a few minutes' conversation with Peter, I am made aware that he is perfectly content with his lot, and above all thoughtful. Yet although he is ceaselessly active in the performance of his camp orderlies, he is doubtless as proficient in the art of enforced idleness as is possible in a man not yet twenty-five years of age.

We go up to the camp which is high on the braeside, and watch the fitful rainstorm sweep across the valley. Presently a stalwart from Glasgow (not far distant), who has apparently some connection with the locomotive workshops, joins us at our supper. This fellow whose name is Rufus can eat a breadloaf at a sitting, and my young host does not fall far short in the matter of appetite.

We discuss Scottish Nationalism, beer, and how to live on ten shillings a week. The evening passes apace. We have achieved an alternative to communism in that we do not try to be what we are not, but like each other for what we are. We sit up late with the flaps of the tent open—talking.

Dusk has long since drawn the veil of night over the distant Bens, before the plate-layer (for such I discover is big Rufus's particular job) consults his watch and makes off for his own tent.

Peter's tent is a large one, but it has to serve many purposes, and after our social evening there is

C

much which could be effected in the interests of tidiness.

Nevertheless, how much better than living all through the summer in a tenement over some darkened " Close." Peter has escaped from all this, and perhaps is more fortunate than some others in that he can provide himself with the things a man needs to make life bearable, and also in that he has a mother who cares how he fares at the braeside camp fourteen miles from the Second City.

I have worked in the industrial areas, when trade has been at its worst, and therefore I am not altogether ignorant of the ravages of unemployment. I have seen there enough of that hollow-eyed anguish, that haunting fear in the soul of a man when the " job " is suspended, to guess at what " unemployment " must mean to the individual.

One afternoon, trudging along in a poor working district, my attention was held by a group of very wretched men waiting on the kerb outside a tavern. They bore the mark of poor housing, malnutrition and—worst of all evils—enforced idleness. They had their coat collars against the rain, and they stared morosely at the passing traffic. Then, as though an original idea had occurred to him, one of their number left his companions and went to the door of the tavern where there was a clock.

" Noo boys," he said, " stop yer bletherin ! Five o'clock and hauf a croon for beer."

So then I knew for the first time that the bars were open at five !

" Can you explain just exactly why you live up here ? " I ask Peter when we are both settled for the night—he on a trestle bed, and I on my mattress on the floor.

"Chiefly because the camp always gives me something to do," he replies ; which answer sends my mind back on the unemployment question again.

After that there is nothing more to be said, and Peter reaches out for the lamp and blows it out. Even so, the light outside, though faint, is sufficient for me to distinguish every detail inside the tent. All at once I realise that I have never been in quite such an unusual lodging before. The humour of the situation takes my fancy, and I involuntarily burst out laughing. Peter, out of sheer good humour, is bound to laugh too, and so in merriment sleep eventually overtakes us.

There are three more scenes with incidental music from the scrap book of " other days."

I had come to St. Fillans at the easterly extremity of Loch Earn. St. Fillans is called after the sixth century leper saint of that name who, after his missionary travels in Scotland, came at last to dwell by the waters of Loch Earn. He could not have chosen a more beauteous place for rest, consolation and shelter from the storms of life.

It was Thursday evening—the occasion of the mid-week service re-layed from St. Michael's, Chester Square. I had my wireless on a house boat anchored on the southern bank of the Loch, and as the organ spoke in the utter stillness of the summer night, people out in skiffs fishing, drifted nearer.

The Reverend W. H. Elliot began his discourse, and soon those silent drifters had no thought of fishing. They drew in their oars, their boats became pews, the house boat was the rostrum, the craggy mountains were the edifice of the temple. " Praise to the Holiest in the Heights, and in the depths be Praise."

The following night I had pitched my tent on a high bank above the River Leny, and I sat up until midnight tending a wood fire and listening to music. Just then the full moon rose, turning a quiet world into a fairyland of exquisite loveliness.

Tempted by the favourable conditions, I collected my towel and soap, and descended to the river to take my customary bath. After my ablutions I swam to mid-stream. The water was unbelievably warm. Suddenly from an adjoining hayfield came ringing shouts and laughter, the woodland glade re-echoed with merriment, as five young men raced for the river.

They stood for a moment on the brink (who should be the first to dare ? ), their statues more animate with natural grace than all the artistry of the Louvre. They plunged.

I rolled in the water like a lazy porpoise playing at a harbour mouth.

" Who's that ? " they asked each other, surprised to find the Leny tenanted at midnight.

" You passed my camp, what of it ? " I replied.

" That's your fire then, we saw the smoke of it from our camp by the farm."

My feet found the pebbly beach, and I hoisted myself out by a projecting branch. The branch broke under my weight, which served my purpose for I fed it to the fire.

By the time that I was dry and had decided to sleep out all night by the fragrant ashes, the bathers were returning across the field; yet before their white forms disappeared from view they turned and hailed me—" Good-night, sleep well."

I slept by the fire, and above me through the trellis-work of the branches I could watch the pageantry of the Heavens. The joy of living was mine.  .  .  .  .  .  .  .

Sleeping out in the open is the best possible tonic to help one to get at the truth of certain matters. Trees, the night wind, stars—the cheery glow of camp fire. What service with bell and pew can compare with this great communion of the out-of-doors?

Years ago in a station waiting-room of a very dismal little town somewhere South, I remember my attention being wholly absorbed by a poster depicting a camp fire built on a high plateau among the Rockies. I remember that the picture made me feel that it was quite necessary to cross the Atlantic in order to know the romance of a camp fire out in the wilds. I thought then that the best attempt at a camp fire seen in Britain was a few cinders kept together in an iron brazier. But I now know that this is not the case.

I also know that in the case of Scout camps at least, a genuine camp fire is not contrived, solely, for the quite legitimate purpose of keeping people warm, although the warmth may be incidental. No, a camp fire should be a ceremonial, and the idea underlying this ceremony is that those members of the camp who have an abundance of energy may get rid of some of it by singing themselves hoarse, and that those who may be a trifle shy can join in, and so each may prove to his neighbour that he too is very much alive and anxious to enjoy himself.

Once at Crieff, I was the guest at such a camp fire.

Imagine ! The light has faded from the Grampians, and the line of mountains shows only as an irregular edge against the last pure light of day. The night steals down. I turn on my wireless, and, marvellous in its defined rhythm, a dance orchestra is serenading the first star of evening.

After which anyone not in the know, might think that something sinister were afoot ! Small boys, who have earlier been playing about in any old clothes, reappear shrouded in blankets—grotesque shapes which hover hither and thither like gnomes.

The fire is blazed, and they squat in a ring at a respectful distance, the ruddy glow throwing their happy faces into strong relief. Gradually, the warmth from the fire gets into everyone's blood, and songs are started.

Then Sandy joins the group. Sandy at once takes command of the proceedings, not because he is a senior, but because he can sing, and enjoy singing. Under his leadership there is harmony and concerted effort. The " Bonnie Banks of Loch Lomond " is our favourite hymn, and a wave of patriotism stirs their Scottish hearts, so that I am quite carried away by it, and entertain a suspicion that I ought to be burnt as an intruder, as a Sassenach . . . . . It is all very good fun.

I glance at my watch and see that it is just on midnight. I touch the switch of my radio and, after a moment's suspense, Big Ben ushers in another day. A hush falls as the bell strikes, and all is so peaceful that the chiming is the only sound in the Universe.

The supper which followed was a simple affair

with cocoa out of tin mugs. Across the river on the braeside were the lights of the Hydro and the lesser lights of Crieff itself. Some of the people in the hotels and boarding-houses must have been late in going to bed. But I am quite certain, on looking back, that we campers had had a better time out under the stars, than the visitors who had spent the evening in dancing or anchored to a card table. For if there is a more perfect entertainment for a summer night than Camp Fire, I have yet to hear of it.

## ON HISTORY AND POLITICS.

A GREAT many books written about Scotland
are concerned, and rightly so, with her past.
If the visitor to Scotland can go to Bannock-
burn near Stirling, to the Pass of Killiecrankie, to the
bottle dungeon of St. Andrews, or to the Border
Keeps, and take with him vivid historical impressions,
I cannot doubt but that his experience is more rich
than if he had not delved into history.

Personally, however, I can enjoy the romance
of a Border Castle without being told that the vaulted
room at the very top of the spiral stair was where the
former kinsmen prepared molten lead to pour down
on the heads of English aggressors. Likewise, while
I am passionately loyal to the memory of great
monarchs like Queen Victoria, I can enjoy a view in
my own way with complete satisfaction without
knowing that Queen Victoria had exclaimed at its
beauty.

But while the history of the past may be read
marked, learned, and digested if possible ; the music
of the past is for ever new, because it can be re-created,
and so, while reminding us of half-forgotten things,
can give us a further measure of joy in the life which
we live to-day.

To listen to many people talking about the
present, is to receive an impression that the destiny
of the human race is entirely in the hands of the

particular Political Party in which they are interested. It would surely be so much easier at least to get along with everybody, if there was a general endeavour to place the interests of the Nation before that of the Party.

It is not a perfect world, but if every individual were prepared to play even an unimportant part in the symphony of communal well-being, it would be a better one. An individual may like to imagine himself as the brass-hatted conductor of the orchestra, but if he is more suited to a back bench let him go there gladly.

For the nation, like the orchestra, depends for its harmony on the perfect co-operation of the whole ; and in the same way the group attains power just so soon as it acknowledges that it is part of the whole.

Again, some high-spirited people believe that any authority imposed from without will keep them on a string, but, if they are being really useful in their own sphere, they will very soon find that that very string which they at first so much resented, has become the rope which will pull them to the top of the mountain.

All this really amounts to a willingness to work. At the fruit harvest all manner of people make a holiday of doing work which is entirely new to them. Their work consists of picking berries. Their hands and arms become stained by fruit juice, but they get tanned by the sun, and are paid for the amount of fruit which they pick. In doing this they are helping to provide the necessities of life for their neighbours.

For my own part I willingly accept the responsibility of work and the inspiration of sentiment.

Sentiment embraces every sphere of compassion, and is the life force which carries idealism and enthusiasm for an ideal to a logical conclusion.

The further I go along the road, and the more people I meet by the wayside, the more certain I become that my neighbour may need me, as I need him.

# I KNOW A ROAD.

I CANNOT imagine what possessed me ever to go to Campbeltown. Kinlochleven is the northern extreme of the County of Argyll, while Campbeltown at the foot of the Mull of Kintyre, is the most southerly point.

Campbeltown is quite a big town, and there is rather a fine harbour.    At the time of my visit there is a regular service of passenger-carrying æroplanes connecting with Glasgow and the mainland.    A little way off is a place called Machrihanish (which I have not visited) much frequented for golf.

Campbeltown seens to me to be strangely akin with Ireland.    I can hear the brogue of the Irish tongue as I pass the entrance of a close.    I have not been enjoying myself, but to-day I have had a sunny walk by the waterside, and observed a gannet striking for herring.    There was not much else to observe.

It is a long road from Oban to Campbeltown. On the way before Tarbert there are four salt water lochs—Loch Feochan, Loch Melfort, Loch Craignish, and wonderful Loch Fyne.    After Tarbert the road south to Campbeltown enters upon the Mull of Kintyre.    Tarbert (which must not be confused with Tarbet on Loch Lomond) is a fishing village, and so essentially primitive, that I do not regret my fleeting impression of it.

As I was driving down the west side of the Mull,

I saw my ideal of a country home. There was a quaint stone bridge over a trickling burn, a cow grazed in green pastures bright with gorse bushes; and the waters of the Loch played at the foot of the cottage garden. Beyond was the eternal grandeur of the hills.

Now the roadway on the east side of the Mull of Kintyre is a mountainous one. At the commencement near Campbeltown is a warning board with the inscription " This road is dangerous throughout." Taking this road on my northwards journey from Campbeltown I stopped to have tea with a family who typify all that is truest and most admirable in Highland courtesy. My host—serene in well-worn kilt— appeared like an oil-painting of his ancestors come to life; while the local doctor, to whom I had the pleasure of being introduced, cut a quaint figure with his red whiskers and monstrous spotted tie.

And so from Campbeltown to Inveraray, the smallest County town in Britain, which I reach at sunset. The mellow pealing of the bells of *All Saints* is utterly in accordance with the atmosphere of calm which prevails here.

Inveraray has all the elusive charm of Scotland, and at the same time the gay flower-patch radiance of England at its best. Beyond the white, red and grey houses of the little town stands the Castle. The rhododendron bushes and wild hyacinths in the grounds would inevitably reduce any artist to tears should he have left his materials behind him. Then there is the restful sight of the swans asleep on the Loch. What a walk for a summer's evening, when

Nature everywhere has painted with such a lavish hand !

There is a cargo steamer at the pier putting in for the night. Having nothing in particular to do with myself, I cross the plank which takes me on deck, and eventually find my way to the stokehold where the stokers are damping down the furnaces for the night.

The heat below is intense, and I learn that the men start work at an hour when the first flush of dawn sees most people blissfully asleep. Also, I gather from their conversation that life would definitely not be worth living without tobacco.

I have, by the way, often wondered at this passionate acclamation of the delights of pipe and cigarettes. Writers maintain, I believe, that tobacco is conducive to thought. But I really believe that both pen wielders and shovel wielders, like a lot of other people I know, take to the soothing influence of the " weed " to console them for anything and everything in life which is denied them. I admit that this is, in part, true of myself ; but cigarettes, however welcome, will never do me the least good, much less induce the harmony of life which some of the victims of tobacco would lead us to believe.

On the other hand, if I were compelled to spend the greater part of my days shovelling coal on a cargo steamer, I am sure that the idea of denying myself so innocent an indulgence as cigarettes would be furthest from my intentions. I had a packet of cigarettes with me when I entered the stokehold, and now, as I have given them away, I shall go to bed without smoking, and in consequence I shall be the more acutely aware of the sweetness of the night.

I finally arrived in Dunoon on a wet Friday. Even so, I liked it from the first. Certainly, I have not experienced Dunoon during the Glasgow Fair Week, when so many of her citizens make their annual excursion " doon the watter ; " nor have I seen Dunoon thronged with the full-tide of August holiday-makers.

But come with me for a while on a soft summer's evening in late May out over the Clyde, in the company of a terribly romantic lady who offered very kindly to row me to the Gantocks Lighthouse.

It is the last evening on which I can go out and hear the nightingales broadcast. My companion and I carry the little boat down to the water's edge, and push off over its calm depths. She sighs a little at the poignant thought of some absent lover, and resigns herself to the oars.

A new moon has risen in a rain-washed sky, and behind us is the dark bulk of the Cowal Hills. There is no sound save the dip of the oars. The coast recedes. Lights from the houses pattern the water with golden beams ; the statue of Highland Mary comes into sight, and it would be difficult to conceive of a silhouette of greater charm. There is the gentle rhythm of the boat as she rides the tiny waves.

I have my wireless beside me, and all at once we are listening to nightingales singing in the Berkshire woods.

The British Broadcasting Corporation has assured us listeners that these are " wild nightingales in their natural surroundings." Personally, it gives me absolutely no pleasure to hear birds singing in any surroundings other than those which are natural to them. Yet to listen just when and how it pleases me, and to know that the nightingales are as free as I am and far more so, is among the most satisfying delights I have ever rejoiced in.

Yachts and yachtsmen are going to bed. We drift close to one of them, and as the nightingales are " faded out " a dance band crooner serenades the owner with a charming little ditty—" Her name is Mary." Further yachtsmen appear on deck, and for all they know we might be lovers ; but in reality we have only the night, and our own thoughts very far away indeed. Even so, I verily believe that we are as happy as the nightingales who have been singing to us in Berkshire.

We glide out to the Gantocks Lighthouse, but are so enraptured with the wonder of the night that somewhat reluctantly the boat is turned for home. At last the keel grates on the shingle, and we tug and pull her to safe anchorage well above high water mark. And Mistress Moon bids our dreams goodnight.

\*     \*     \*     \*     \*     \*

Since writing the foregoing I have been interviewed by a local gossip writer. Perhaps unfortunately I told him about my little jaunt on the Clyde, and a subsequent issue of his paper has devoted two paragraphs to the incident.

I find myself described as a " Wireless Fiend," and I append an extract from one of the paragraphs.

" A young man who was resident in Dunoon for a few days, was out in a rowing boat after dark one

evening. . . . . . He delights in taking his portable
set on a boat while he can listen while watching—
as he says—' the new moon rising in a rain-washed
sky ! ' Readers will have judged that he is rather
sentimental and fond of dramatic situations. He is
—he's English."

Of course, the sensible Englishman usually lets
the silent emotional Scot enjoy his little joke in peace ;
and I have certainly enjoyed this one immensely.

In any case, I am far too grateful for the generous
co-operation of newspapers all over the country in
reporting obscure and occasionally poorly-attended
meetings, to harbour any ill-will against them.

Later this self-same newspaper has come out
with the startling heading " Dunoon Lecturer Hits
Out at Vivisection," and so what can I do, more
especially after having addressed " a very large
audience " which was indeed a statement of fact,
but congratulate them on their sense of news value !

If the meetings are well reported, the gossip
writers can say what they like in their diaries. It
would be a dull world if we took everything too
seriously and forgot how to laugh. Not many people
can make a joke, but a great number of people can
laugh—which is very much better for all of us.

It is Sunday evening. I am sitting alone in a
sun porch writing. Gardens gay with flowering
shrubs slope down to the West Bay. Already the
rowing boats have been beached for the night, and
one by one the lights begin to show from neighbouring houses. There is a pleasure steamer out on the
Firth coming in from a Sunday trip to the Kyles of
Bute.

Before me I have a letter from a lady who alludes to the " awful terror " which in her childhood she experienced on seeing these " Sabbath breakers," as she then regarded Sunday steamer trips, or apparently Sunday trips of any kind.

I wonder what she would think if she came over to see me one of these bright Sundays, and looked—only " looked " of course—at the neat row of inviting motor charabancs which will transport anyone by the friendly banks of Loch Eck, or elsewhere in the wonderland of Argyll mountains which hold Dunoon in their palm. Or again we could—in imagination—board one of the " awful terrors," and see ourselves sitting in deck chairs out of the breeze sailing " doon the watter " to the accompaniment of the ship's band playing snatches of light music.

But as all my best Sundays are spent in disturbing myself as little as is conceivably possible, we should probably not get even as far as thinking about doing anything. As a kind of concession we might spend all the morning on the sun terrace, and then in the afternoon walk as far as the Holy Loch, where there is enough interesting craft lying at anchor to prove an absorbing study to the most land-lubbing landsman. In the evening I fancy we should idle to the little church on the hill.

Being alone, however, I have not been a walk all this Sunday, except towards evening I have been down to the pier and watched kilted hikers embarking for Glasgow.

Most of them had been camping in the hills during Saturday night, probably near a farmhouse, where they supplied their simple wants. They had

D

been spending Sunday where there are streams and woods.

I went so far as to envy them their week-end. So having tried the reflective Sunday, I herewith determine to be idle next Sunday without the effort of reflection, and I shall require only my tent, the sun in his heaven, trees and a stream with bathing in a clear pool. I determine to go back to the sun.

## SUNDAY IN THE HILLS.

THERE is a village called Clachaig near Dunoon up the Glen Road which would take you, if you pursued it long enough, to the head of Loch Striven, and further to Glendaruel and Otter Ferry on Loch Fyne.

It is worth while being in a Highland Glen at four in the morning, if only to make believe that you are alone in a wonderful world with only the birds and beasts for company. For there is only one thing more delightful than the song of birds at sunset, and that is their song at dawn. I stand a little way from the tent watching a water wag-tail preening himself; and close at hand a robin hops contentedly.

When a new day comes in the solitude of the hills, the soft light mellows their form, and surely reveals them in their true beauty. The sun sets nature aflame after the dawn, even as a woman's love for a man can change and beautify his character. In the morning all things are renewed.

At last the sun rides high in the sky—the hour of worship and wonder is past—and in its place comes the ecstatic delight of being alive under a cloudless sky; of searching for and finding a pool high up the burn, a pool into which an elfin waterfall cascades from overhanging rocks. Thus splashing in childlike caprice, stretching luxuriously on the grassy bank, once or twice exploring the braeside for exercise, I let the idle hours of noon merge themselves into the subdued lonely hours of evening; I let the day slip into the night which is the hour of music if not of revelry.

Returning to my tent, I open my wireless in time to hear the opening bars of a favourite symphony, and then creep into my bed on the good earth to snuggle down to listen to music in a world of stillness.

It has been a great day this peaceful Sunday, and when the sun shines at Whitsuntide, one feels it is a good omen for the summer that is in store. Later, as I lay me down to sleep, a text from the Book recurs to my mind. It is this, " The glory of this latter house shall be greater than that of the former, and in this place will I give peace."

## HAUD WEST.

NO one could be more sorry than I to leave the Clyde, to bid good-bye to the yachts which, when in full sail on the Firth, look like white butterflies with folded wings. I shall be sorry to leave all the friendly people, sorry to see the last of the tinkers who have been living on the coast near Innellan gathering whelks. As I lie awake at night perhaps by the side of a burn, I shall hear their talk and laughter in the murmur of it.

My road to Mull is to take me right through the heart of Argyll, by Loch Eck, Glen Arary, Portsonachan and Dalmally and thus to Oban. And my first camp is near Ardbrecknish House at Portsonachan on Loch Awe.

Portsonachan is a Gaelic word and means literally " Haven of Peace." I am camping in a farm field overlooking the Loch, where the wild iris grows down by the spinney which borders the water. The tent is set to overlook the Loch ; and a little walk to Arbrecknish private pier convinces me that Loch Awe, for all her forbidding moods must, in her stark beauty and alluring grace, claim first place in my affections above all other lochs.

I am perfectly happy in the Highlands without wishing to foregather with the people who come to Scotland for the fishing and the shooting. It is unfortunate that the impression has been spread abroad that the Highlands of Scotland are the exclusive preserve of those who wish to show forth their dexterity, or lack of it, with rod and gun.

The only sport of which I see evidence at Portsonachan is that of motor speed-boating on the Loch. If I were to be aboard the boat, I fancy that I should find more genuine thrill in being one with her mad career, than I did in the poetic effortless ease of " straight " flying. Should there be an element of danger so much the better.

Speed on the water seems to suggest a novelty greater than that of speed on land or aloft. For instance, if one travels at speed in a motor car on anything but a racing track, the thrill is liable to prove a menace to one's fellow-men. Again, if one goes in for " straight " flying, especially in a passenger aeroplane, the element of thrill centres around the fact that one is flying, rather than in the fact of travelling from one place to another at not less than a hundred miles an hour.

Yes, I could imagine that a holiday at Portsonachan might be very enjoyable, and if there was the chance of trying out a speed-boat on the Loch, I can foresee that the holiday would be not only enjoyable but also exhilarating.

The following morning there is a little mist on the mountain until the sun is strong enough to dispel it. I am beginning to think that there is nothing in all the earth more kindly, more fair than this beautiful place until, on my way to thank the farmer for giving me the ground, I pass a cart-shed with wide open doors and within from a high beam there hangs by a rope the body of a newly-killed sheep. So, unknown to me, they had been doing this thing at dawning at the haven of peace.

My second camp on the road back to Oban is at Strae Bridge, by Dalmally, and the scene has a background of wild mountains suggestive of Wagner's " Ride of the Valkyrie" graven in stone. I hear the plaintive call of the curlew, and I am reminded by an old farmer with whom I get into conversation, that in bygone days clans were called together by imitating the call of certain birds.

Among rocks a little way up the stream, I find an almost perfect natural bath. The wayside bath is never more refreshing to the wayfarer than when he has covered many roadways in the glaring heat of a day in June.

## THE FOOT OF THE ROCK.

THE prevailing and certainly the most popular time to set out on a journey in the Highlands is six o'clock in the morning. Thus it is that I find myself on a grey Monday morning aboard the six o'clock steamer bound for Mull.

Oban harbour is soon left behind, and with the gulls following us, we pass by the battleships lying at anchor in the Firth, and it is not long before we have our first near glimpse of Mull in Duart Castle, the feudal home of the clan MacLean.

Landing in Tobermory, which is in the north of the Island, I borrow a bicycle, and set 'off up hill and down dale to Salen. Salen is further south; a few boats call there from Oban, but perhaps if I had taken one of these and landed at Salen, I should not have been so fortunate in being lent a really excellent bicycle.

Further along, hard by Loch Ba, there is, I believe, an estate which is a sanctuary for animals, and it is at the tiny post office, on the road here, that I learn that a friend and his wife are camping on the coast at Gribun, Loch na Keal.

Gribun is a far cry to pay a call, and of all desolate roadways which I have ever traversed, that on the south side of Loch na Keal must remain with me as the most memorable. There does not appear to be a house in sight for miles. Occasionally, I dismount from my machine to listen, and each time I do so (although I know it is but fancy) I can hear the distant echo of pipes, as though the haunted solitudes voiced a deathless dirge.

I have reached Gribun which means in the Gaelic the foot of the rock. On the one side of the roadway, which is but a few feet above the Loch, tower the Gribun rocks. The water reflects them as jade green crags in a sea of glass. I feel that I might as well have been cast up on the face of the moon.

Gribun has but three houses. The first is a white-washed fisher's cottage, from the door of which I can see a green tent down by the shore which is the object of my pilgrimage. The tent is pitched down on a grassy peninsula : a perfect situation most obviously chosen by an expert eye.

I am told by the good lady at the cottage that the campers are away for the day, and that they will not be expected back until quite late in the evening.

Gribun is the " clachan " of the clan MacFadyen, I am among Gaelic-speaking people, yet how pleasing is their English diction ! They are bi-lingual in the true sense of the word, for when they speak to one another, it is in the Gaelic, the language of their fore-elders.

Mrs. MacFadyen very kindly arranges for me to stay the night at the white cottage, and I am shown into a room which is really far more in line with modern ideas than I had expected. On the centre table stands the " Firoran Games Challenge Cup for the best local athlete." On examining it I see that in 1927 it was awarded to one Neil M'Lean, but that in 1928 and 1929 it was won by John MacFadyen, and so apparently was permitted to become an heirloom in the family.

After a while my friends came down the road in an open motor. They have a dog with them. They have been having a wonderful day enriching their collection of photographs of bird-life. I inwardly congratulate them on being able to *afford* to ship a motor with them to the Isles, for such is not an undertaking lightly to be considered. We talk about every thing, except the wonder of the scene which surrounds us, and then they are away back to the little green tent and I to the white cottage at the foot of the rock.

It is the evening hour, and I sit outside the house with the family and watch the lights over the Loch change with the setting sun.

Mr. MacFadyen senior has a fund of stories.

"Once upon a time," he begins, and I will endeavour in my own words to re-tell two of his stories.

Once upon a time, then, there was a shepherd who lived out on a neighbouring island, who came to Gribun to take unto himself a wife, and also to tend the flocks in the district.

The wedding was accompanied by much merry-making, and while the guests were disporting themselves to the skirl of the pipes, the young couple stole away to their new home which was close to the hall where the guests made merry. All was as it should be until an unkind fate took a hand in the matter, for during the night a great boulder dislodged itself from the rocks above, and fell on the house which the newly-weds had but so recently made their home. The guests were, however, either too merry or too drunk to hear the disturbance, and so it was not until

the morning that they knew of the disaster at all!
This, in spite of the fact that the boulder was of such
dimensions as to completely obliterate the cottage,
so that only a few posts protruded from under it.

The boulder to which Mr. MacFadyen alludes
is not far from the white cottage; and as we walk
over to view it, he shows me the foundations of several
former dwelling-houses, which I gather were pulled
down at some not very remote period, but for what
precise reason I am unable to understand. All the
same, it must have been a strange village, for I am
informed that sixty-three years ago there was not even
a road leading to it.

As we walk back to our seats by the cottage door
another story begins to unfold itself.

Now it happened that a little corn grew down
by the coast, and it was said that a terrible monster
would rise out of the deep to despoil it. Moreover,
all those who had seen the monster declared that its
body was full of fire and was therefore no creature of
this earth.

The riddle might have remained unsolved, and
the nightly plunderings of corn might have continued,
had it not been for a certain young man chancing all
unawares upon the simple fact that the fiery monster,
which had inspired so much dread and dark foreboding,
was nothing more terrible than a bull from the island
of Inch Kenneth.

This intrepid young man would on Thursday
of each week, summer and winter, swim from the
coast of Mull by Clachandhu to Inch Kenneth in
order to pay his respects to the lassie whom he courted
most ardently. It was a summer's evening and,

stripping, he placed his clothes as usual to carry on his head while he swam the dividing strait, a distance of perhaps half a mile. When he was a little way out from Clachandhu, he saw a dark head in the water making rapid progress towards the coast which he had just left. Curious, he swam towards the object, to behold a bull rise from the water. On landing the bull shook itself, and its matted coat being full of phosphorescent water, it appeared to his startled vision that the creature's body was full of fire. But being a sensible young man he was not at all alarmed, and on the following day he was easily able to dispel the apprehensions regarding the unearthly " monster " which had visited his kinsfolk.

I think it must be because of the spirit of mystery and the power of mystic thought which prevails in the Isles as much as the evidence of interesting flora and fauna found there, that makes them such an unfailing source of interest to Scottish writers. And I have heard people whose ancestors hailed from Skye, speak of the " Misty Isle " with baited breath, as though the wonder of it might not be guessed by those who had not trod the Coolins as pilgrims in a holy land.

Before leaving Gribun there is only one other fact that I wish to set down about it, because I take it to be typical of the whole of the far-flung Highlands. The fact is that you need not lock your door at night ; nor do you, perhaps you have nothing in your possession worth taking, and you can rest secure in the knowledge that no one wishes to take anything from you whether it is of value or not. In the Highlands, every man is a friend.

I rise early in the morning, and I am in time to

see my friend bathe from his tent with the company
of his ever-faithful collie. There is a nice clean
beach, and the two of them enjoy their plunge tremen-
dously.

By nine o'clock I am saying good-bye to the
MacFadyens, and pursue the sandy, stony roads back
to Tobermory.

Yet when I arrive there, the last steamer for Oban,
which I had hoped to catch, has sailed out of sight
down the Sound ; and the " Lochinvar " is anchored
by the pier-side ready to sail in the morning. Nevertheless, I do my very best to see how I can possibly
reach Oban by nightfall. I find that if I go a tremendous distance in a cargo steamer calling in at the head
of Loch Sunart in Morven, I can walk a tremendous
distance up Glen Tarbert, and then take a ferry
across into Inverness-shire, and another ferry across
into Argyll at Ballachulish. From Ballachulish I
might be lucky in getting a lift down the coast to
Ledaig. I should then cross the Connel Ferry Railway Viaduct and take a 'bus to Oban. I give it up
in despair !

And there is no telephone communication with
the mainland. One can telegraph, of course. The
telegrams pass through Glasgow and thus to their
destinations.

The battleships lie in the bay, and Tobermory
is full of English sailors. I hear as much of the
" cockney " intonation as I might in the Tottenham
Court Road. There is a placard advertising a dance
to which the ladies are to be admitted free.

I take up a lodging for the night in a house with
a very lovely view over the bay. Here, to my great

delight, I discover a gramophone capable of giving an impression of Sir Harry Lauder singing " Keep right on to the end of the road," which delight I share with a clerk on holiday from Glasgow. His real home is Harris, and he tells me a great deal which I did not previously know about the Hebrides. While we are talking we stand at the open sitting-room window and watch the battleships give a display of searchlights. But I am more interested in hearing about the Hebrides, than I am entertained by watching the searchlights. And so, for a few brief hours to bed—a bed which is clean and warm, but entirely innocent of sheets. However, once between the blankets I soon forget my disappointment at not being in Oban by nightfall.

Aboard the " Lochinvar " we have three motor cars as cargo, one of which belongs to my friend of the green tent. He and his wife are taking their car as far as Lochaline, from whence they will explore the beauties of Morven. " Loch Aline " means simply the " beautiful loch."

As we come alongside the pier at Lochaline, the " Lochinvar " lies so low in the water that, in order to land the car, it is necessary to run it up two steeply inclined planks. The gradient is very steep, but under its own power, and with the assistance of a rope, the car attempts it. The first effort is a failure. For one anxious moment everyone on board thinks there will be an accident, but making another rush, the car's own weight tips up the planks and so lands it safely on the pier.

They wave good-bye, and we wish them well. Theirs, no doubt, is a very happy tour, but I am convinced that the best way of travelling in the Islands is not by means of motor car or pedal cycle, but on foot.   And if, when on a holiday, you have not time to walk the island of your dreams, it may, perhaps, be better to stay on the mainland.

## WHO IS MY NEIGHBOUR?

" COULD you face up to nine months without human conversation, with only the communications of the spirit in prayer ? "

The diner opposite me looks at me enquiringly over the cafe table.

" I was in a Monastery for nine months," he continues, " and it was a silent Order. Then I found that I had no Vocation. I drifted out into the world. Tried all sorts of things. You may be surprised, but I am now operating the machine of a Talkie Picture Theatre."

This man's conversation is to me a far more real relaxation than the book which I had brought with me to idle away the period of a solitary luncheon. And the way in which he had introduced himself was so unusual and charming.

I had chosen the table at which we were sitting, simply because there was no table disengaged. The waitress presented the menu. I ran my eye over the various dishes, but finding that the little cafe made no effort to provide a single vegetarian dish, I had simply ordered vegetables.

" Excuse me," the little man had said, " but if there's any difficulty about settling the account, I should be only too pleased . . . . I know what these days are you know."

His sincerity was so obvious, and his failure to

understand why I should merely require to eat vegetables interested me. Thereafter our conversation
has moved forward on a delicious voyage of contrast-
ing experiences.

"Did you follow what I meant by the 'Discipline,' when I alluded to it just now?" he asks at
length.

"No, I'm afraid I didn't."

"Well, there are times, and you must have
experienced them yourself, when the flesh has to be
brought into subjection. For instance, nearly everyone lies an unduly long time in bed in the mornings
whenever there is a chance to do so. A perhaps un-
wise generalization, I admit, but it would be better
for those who did so if they rose and prayed. It would
at least be a form of 'discipline' that would save
them from the hopeless morass of indulgence and
self-love.

"Our Monastic 'Discipline' consisted of worship at three in the morning. Each Brother carried
a knotted cord, and bearing his back by letting down
his habit to the waist, would belabour himself according to his own desires. You will be able to appreciate
now the significance of the well-known Biblical
passage 'I buffet my body and beat it into bondage
lest when I have preached to others I, myself, should
be a castaway.'"

This reasoning is very pleasing, and I am
beginning to appreciate a great many things which,
previously, I have hardly considered at all.

"And is this self-imposed 'Discipline' merely a
ritual or a genuine infliction?" My remark verges

E

on the curious, but my new friend does not rebuff me on that account.

"Yes, sometimes our 'Discipline' was what you would term a 'genuine infliction.' But the Brothers were always most careful not to make a display of their self-punishment. When one of our number found blood on the knotted cord, he would endeavour to cleanse it in the wash-house without being observed."

There is a pause in our conversation, and my companion orders coffee for two.

"Surely there were Brothers in your Order who felt that they could do good by writing a book," I suggest, "even if they foreswore the exchange of conversation?"

"Books are written," the other returns, "but always in the seclusion of the individual cell. They enter the cell to write their book, and food is brought to them. When the pages are filled, the book is handed through the grating, so that during the whole period of the work, there can be no possible intrusion from the outside world.

"I was not among those who sought to do good by writing a book, but each of us, according to our ability, did good in other ways. After a time we became used to the silence. But unless one has an unswerving Vocation, you will understand. . . . Anyway here I am doing a perfectly good job, everything is new as though I had truly entered another life during those nine months. You see, before I decided to adopt the Monastic life, I gave away everything I possessed except the clothes in which I walked the streets, so that when I came back I had to make a start all over again. The experience has taught me many things."

I am already very late over my lunch, and so, still talking, I take my account to the cash desk, and pass with the ex-monk down the stairs and out into the street.

I am sorry to part with him. It is comparatively rare to meet with anyone whose society is uplifting, while there are any amount of people of a slightly morbid character whose sub-conscious influence is anything but helpful. But here was someone who made his own way in life, and who, at the same time, most obviously found opportunities for helping other people to make their way.

I watch him down the street. There is someone at the corner begging, and yes, I was sure of it, he does not walk past without giving as do most of the passers-by.

And I am sure that the word and the smile which will accompany the gift will mean something to the beggar even if the sum received is not a very large one.

He has returned to the world, and many, I venture to hope, will be glad of it.

I invariably find it easy to write of pleasant people I like. There is Jock now who has come for a period to relieve me of a few of my many duties. He is a realist, but all his realism is idealism. To use a Scots expression, he " keeps a body frae languor." But he gives his friendship, so far as I am able to discover, only to animals.

We are camping in a stackyard at a village some way from Helensburgh, and it is quite amazing to observe the kindly consideration which Jock shows to the poorest member of the farmyard zoo. Even should a chicken roost on his bed during the night (a not uncommon occurrence where there are poultry about, and the flaps of the tent are allowed to remain unfastened) he will not object. The fellow is, too, excellent company, so that if you were talking with him you would never suspect that he prefers the companionship of a Cairn terrier to your companionship or that of anyone else. He seems to befriend all animals, but if he has a preference among them, I understand that it would be horses, elephants, dogs —in that order.

Jock is a young individualist in the early twenties, of Scottish and Irish parentage. He wears the kilt with a certain amount of distinction, and his Balmoral, which has seen a lot of service, bears the letters " R.S." which is the designation of the Rover Scouts.

In many ways he is the Scot of the Music Halls—light-hearted, amusingly independent. Yet on further acquaintance it is found that most of his chaff serves only to disguise the nobler issues of a nature quixotically generous. His philosophy of life is perhaps best expressed in the cheery song with which he will enliven a long road home, or the stolid indifference with which he greets the prospect of getting up in the rain.

Incidentally, I find that camping for three weeks in a stackyard occasions me quite a lot of diversion and interest. I like observing at close quarters the habits of poultry. I enjoy the companionship of the horses, and I enjoy the company of Kelpie, the collie dog.

Moreover, very early in our stay I came to know

Mistress MacDougall who lives at the farm bothy
with her husband and young son. She it was who
made an overture of friendship by providing Jock
and myself with very delicious and substantial home-
made scones. Mistress MacDougall is a little
puzzled that I have not served my time at a " trade,"
but otherwise I see that I am fast becoming an
addition to her social circle.

Hugh Vincent Cassels Alexander MacKenzie
was among our first visitors. It has transpired that
his father would simply have given his son the one
name of Hugh ; but as this boy was the first child
to be baptized by a new minister after his advent to the
Parish, he received the minister's names in addition,
thus conforming to an old Scots custom.

I think that I should also say something about
the farmer with whom we are camping. He is a man
of honour, leisure and position, and he kindly allows
us to make a home in his stackyard without charge.

The other day Jock worked at the haymaking.
He must have given satisfaction, for afterwards Mr.
Farmer came up to me and said significantly " Jock's
a good man," which remark I took to imply " it would
be nice to see *you* doing something useful occasionally."

I should, of course, find it a pleasure to make hay,
but perhaps Mr. Farmer does not realise that I could
hardly leave my work in order to do so. I do not
think that either he or Mistress MacDougall know that
some people do *work* with their coats on, their hair
brushed, and return from their " day's darg " (as
we say in Scotland) without showing outward signs
of having worked at all.

Incidentally, the Irishwomen and their menfolk who are " imported " to help at busy times are, I am told, very good workers. One of the men spoke to me to-day, and told me that he was suffering from a nervous breakdown and that he had not " snored to sleep " for the past three months. The poor fellow's face was considerably swollen after having a tooth out, but although I was naturally intensely sorry that he should be suffering so much discomfort, I could scarce repress a smile when he informed me that he had been " debolished after having a tooth sub-tracted." How many of us have been " debolished " by a similar ordeal !

The Irish are notoriously a musical people, and no day is complete for these sons of the soil unless it ends with song—usually to the accompaniment of a mouth-organ. One evening when two of the men were working about the stackyard, an orchestra over my wireless struck up the " Londonderry Air."

Instantly, the workers paused in whatever they were doing, and their eyes had a far-away look as though they were thinking of home, as I have no doubt was indeed the case.

Subsequently, my portable wireless set has been held in great regard, and now in the evenings the Irish folk will sometimes sit round near the camp listening to music of every description. Like me, they must be quite indiscriminate in their musical taste. Personally, I appreciate music of all kinds, even as the open-air man takes the weather as it comes, welcoming with equal joy the rain, the frost and the sunshine.

It is quite an easy thing for many people to

appreciate music of all kinds, but it is harder for some to make the most of the companionship of their neighbours whoever they are. I am sceptical about the people who go out into a world of loveliness in order to " escape." What are they escaping from ? They cannot escape from themselves.

Mr. J. J. Bell in his book " Scotland's Rainbow West " suggests that the immortal Dr. Johnson is an example to all travellers, since he made the best of comfort as well as discomfort ; and although I could by no means describe a farmyard camp as discomfort, it must certainly be accounted a very simple but by no means despicable habitation. And further I am sure that the normal individual can enjoy living (if he is fit) in the simplest manner imaginable.

Thinking of Dr. Johnson reminds me that many travellers, both in fact and fiction, took a companion with them. Johnson took Boswell, Paul took Barnabas, and the twelve Apostles set out not singly, but in twos. Yet in many ways I would rather be alone, unless a companion could be found who shared my love of animals, joy in music, and neighbourly feelings towards those whom I met by the wayside.

I rather hope that, in time, Jock's sympathies might become as expansive as my own. For instance, when I carelessly leave bread or other provisions where the farmyard ducks can gobble it, and Jock says, " It's an ill wind that blaws naebody guid, ye ken!" I know perfectly well that he does not grudge the duck its morsel which I so richly deserved to lose.

We lay our beds on straw, whereas St. Francis of Assisi would have slept upon the ground. I have a sleeping bag replete with a canvas pillow in a linen slip. Jock has contrived to make a warm quilt into a sleeping bag by the simple expedient of doubling it and sewing it up one side.

A few nights ago when we had both been sleeping for some time, I was awakened by a curious noise which I took to be a rat in the straw with which the ground of the tent is covered.

I shook Jock awake. " Whit's wrang wi' ye, noo ? " he asked sleepily.

" There's a jolly old rat along with us," I suggested.

We moved our beds and searched the straw, but in vain.

It occurred to me that the noise might be coming from outside the tent. Accordingly I took a flashlight and peered outside. There was a hedgehog among our pots and pans, most evidently in search of food.

" Are hedgehogs vegetarians, Jock ? " I enquired.

" I canna mind," he said, " but gi'e it bread an' cheese. And if you're nae sleeping the nicht, I am. Guid-nicht."

## CHEERFUL INTERLUDE.

CALLANDER, St. Fillans, Aberfeldy, Dunkeld, Auchterarder, are names the very sound of which conveys a picture. St. Fillans has too many visitors for my liking, but the gypsies would appear to derive a fair revenue from them. The gypsy sons are taught to play the pipes, and the gypsy daughters sell white heather.

I have often met " Granny," one of the oldest of this nomad tribe. " Granny " has been suffering from a consumptive cough for I don't know how long. She always tells me when she meets me that she knows a kind face when she sees one, which is her little way of asking me to give her as much as I can afford. Frankly, I enjoy giving " Granny " money, a fact of which the old body is well aware.

At St. Fillans Jock and I met a very nice gentleman from Aberdeen, to whom I perhaps unwisely confided some of my little ways of spending money. In reply our friend pointed out that some distinction should be drawn between generosity and extravagance ; and I was inclined to believe him, since he himself appeared to be the soul of kindness. He was on a caravan holiday with his family, and we pitched our camps side by side on the south bank of the Earn.

At this moment we are camping beside the old bridge at Aberfeldy. Jock and I are having a " gran' crack " round the fire.

" Would you consider me unduly extravagant ? "
I ask suddenly.

" Weel, oor frien' frae Aiberdeen thocht ye a saft
boob, an' maybe he was richt ! "

" Yet you know perfectly well that you yourself
would give away your last sixpence, if by so doing you
could be of service to someone."

" Oh, ay ! " he admits, " but I learnt that frae
the auld folks as a bit laddie.   The baith o' them wud
aye be giein' a piece to those that wud itherwise  hae
gane hungry.   Ma faither wud aye gi'e a piece awa'
to ony puir body nae sae well aff as oorsels."

" Of course money isn't everything," I add.
" There's the pleasure of giving someone companionship, of helping someone to believe in himself, and
all that sort of thing."

Jock is engaged in boiling soup in a billy can over
the fire made between bricks.

" There're some things siller canna buy," he says
shortly.

On our way through Perthshire we have met the
" New Tramps "—men of all ages out from the industrial areas in search of work.  They go about in
gangs, asking farmers for jobs, and they sleep about
in barns or perhaps by the wayside.

I am given to understand that they have a sort
of secret society among themselves, and I have no
doubt but that their code of honour is strictly adhered
to.   This development, if such it can be termed, is
the outcome of unemployment, and the subject
would perhaps form an interesting book in itself.

Coming to Dunkeld we are " campit " in the
park at Birnam where the Highland gathering is held.

Here are amazing beechwoods, kissed by the rushing waters of the Tay.

I love Dunkeld, and each time I come to it, I do not fail to admire the quaint street to the right of the city which straggles up the hillside in the wildest abandon. It always seems to me very strange thinking of Dunkeld as a city, for in size it is little more than a village. Above and around are the heather hills, and views of indescribable beauty.

Apart from the fact that my coming to Dunkeld has coincided with the opening of the grouse shooting season, the occasion would be a happy one. I hear that the beaters are out by seven o'clock, and on a big " drive " there will be as many as thirty-five beaters one hundred yards apart.

The shots started depressingly early, but to-morrow being Sunday there will be a truce, and we shall be able to go to the hills in peace.

Sunday, by the way, we largely devote to an expedition in search of white heather. In August the purple heather is in bloom, but it is quite a matter of chance finding *white* heather, and perhaps because it is the thirteenth of the month, our quest does not meet with success.

Jock makes up for the disappointment by bringing back a large armful of purple heather, which he cuts with a sheath knife. Once at the camp, after placing a sprig on the car mascot, he proceeds to pack the heather in a large cardboard box.

" Are you sending that home to Glasgow ? " I hazard.

" Na ! Na ! The heather's no' for the auld folks," he returns. " See here, Paul, I ken a lassie doon at Morecambe wha's fair daft for the sicht o' a bit heather frae amang the hills o' Scotland. Come ben here and tak' a wee peep at her picture."

I examine the photograph at my leisure.

" Is she English ? " I ask.

" Oh, ay ! she's English, but she's a nice piece a' the same ! "

After which complimentary gesture he sinks into a contemplative silence.

Tired after a long walk in the hills, I retire early and soon fall dreamlessly asleep. But Jock is determined to write the girl at least " fower pages," and therefore I am constantly to be roused from slumber by being requested how I spell words like " through " and " thought."

When several appeals have fallen upon my dulled senses, I raise myself on my elbows and protest that I myself do not spell correctly, and that in any case I do not like spelling.

" Maist folks dinna ken hoo to spell," he says doggedly pursuing his Herculean task. " Maybe ye canna spell, but the morn's mornin' ye'll need tae learn hoo to get up ! Ther'll be nae lying a bed for you till ten o'clock. So noo you've been telt ! "

I positively detest getting up early in the morning. Indeed, I find it an absolute bore. Nevertheless, as I had been " telt " to get up early, I get up at seven fifteen.

Let me admit, however, that the getting up is not of my own free will. The alarm clock merely serves to annoy me, and a warning curse from my companion solicits nothing but an unintelligible monosyllable.

Suddenly my sleeping bag is seized at the foot, and I am dragged from the tent " neck and crop " into the out-of-doors. A well-aimed kick completes the good work, and I find myself standing in the bright radiance of the August morning.

To-day I paid a very smart call, on people who are relations of friends. Her Ladyship was resting, and I was asked to wait until she came downstairs.

In the library I found an annotated edition of " Manners for Men," which I found to be a feast of glorious fun. I made a quick mental note of the fact that gentlemen should call between the hours of four and seven in the afternoon.

When at last my hostess came downstairs to receive me, I thought her really very intriguing.

" Excuse me barging in and all that," I murmured.

" I'm only too charmed," she said, "that you thought of looking in on us like this. You must be sure and give Aunt Fanny our love when you see her."

After a while we discovered that we had something in common.

" I hear you're musical," she suggested, " do play me something."

Without reference to " Manners for Men " I was a little uncertain if this invitation was to be taken in good earnest. Perhaps I should have said " Really, you know, I only play for my own amusement, and that only by ear." Or " I studied music abroad at one time, but I'm afraid I simply can't find time to practise now-a-days. Such a frightful bore practising at the piano, don't you think."

However, far from making excuses, I gladly complied with the suggestion, although I have no doubt that the author of a book on etiquette might have indicated a certain deference in so doing.

One cannot have everything in life all at once, and the only thing I sigh for slightly while camping, is not for a piano (although I like playing one whenever there is a chance to do so), but for the opportunity to walk in a rose garden every day. As with a great many other people I have a passion for rose gardens, blue china and embroidered linen, and I do not hesitate to say that I miss rose gardens, and that when I have eaten off enamel plates for four or five months, it is a welcome thing to renew my acquaintance with the Willow Pattern.

And talking of flowers reminds me that during my smart call, I learnt that the "bluebells of Scotland" are harebells, and not wild hyacinths as one might have supposed. Now I like, when I can, to learn something from everybody, so I must regard this call as a great success.

By the evening I have come on a long way for my next camp, which is in juxtaposition to the fifth hole of Gleneagles Golf Course. I am provided with permission to " erect a tent and camp for one night," and as the weather is fine if cold, and as we have a peaceful view over harvest fields and heather-clad hills, there is, as yet, little about which to complain.

Being at the edge of the Golf Course, Jock and I amuse ourselves by watching the approach shots to the fifth hole, and the putting on the green itself.

" Can they folk no' get gowff in England ? " he demands.

"Yes, but as golf is the Scottish national game, every golfer who can, plays golf when he comes to Scotland, and quite right too. I understand they have a preference for Gleneagles or St. Andrews."

"Masel' I wud raither be hain' a game o' fitba'," Jock says obstinately, and I am content to leave it at that, without pursuing the discussion further.

"Aiblins it'll be a gey cauld nicht," he continues, "and here's the first shooer o' rain."

Sure enough the rain is coming, gently at first, and now with merciless intensity. Everything outside has to be hastily collected, and stowed in car and tent.

Being cold in camp is a comparatively rare experience, but a decidedly unpleasant one. Newspapers are splendid to put under and on top of one's bed, but although I do this, I spend most of the night in sheer misery. I lie awake and think.

I recall seeing a wedding party dancing at Gleneagles Hotel, with the men resplendent in the kilt. Then, for no special reason, I begin to wish myself in the warm, almost silent cabin of a luxury air-liner on a flight from Croydon to Paris.

At last I begin to doze, and as I do so it is with the comforting thought that during the winter in Paris, certain small breeds of dogs wear amazing little "tailor-made" coats.

When I wake up in the morning I find that Jock has transferred a blanket from his bed to mine.

"Good heavens," I explain, "weren't you cold in the night?"

"Awa' an' shoot yourself," he returns, "I thocht naething aboot the cauld at a'."

And in spite of the fact that he had been covered only by the single thickness of a quilt, I have to believe him.

## FELLOW-MORTALS.

FELLOWSHIP between man and man is a factor in spiritual development which is widely appreciated. But when we were very young, that is, before we could exchange service for service, and were capable only of an instinctive knowledge of what we wanted, coupled with the art of crying out loudly until we got it, we naturally did not know anything about service for others, the exercise of kindness, or the spirit of good fellowship. If we played with the cat, perhaps we did so exclusively for our own amusement, rather than for the edification of our companion.

Yet if we were gentle by nature, and the cat was wise and forbearing, we did not get scratched, and so perhaps it was born to our untutored mind that we " loved little pussy." Then at a later stage of our development perhaps we found that we not only " loved little pussy " but a great number of other creatures as well. We became their playmates. The child and the animal had found that the bond which existed between them was one of joy in innocent fun.

I really think that it must be the exceptional child who is intentionally cruel. The adolescent can be just as cruel to his own kind as he is to creatures who are entirely helpless, but I would say that no child

F

is ever cruel believing and asserting that cruelty is justified. A good deal has been heard about the child who wilfully mutilates a fly, the child who ties a tin can to a cat's tail and chases it, but while the adult person has some glib excuse for the cruelties he perpetrates, the child is often solely actuated by savage curiosity which, since he knows it to be wrong, he does not seek to excuse.

The " impressionable age " of young people seems to vary a good deal, but sometimes any clear indication of conscious reaction to good influences and bad ones is long delayed. For instance, a natural aversion to injustice of any kind may for years smoulder unrecognised alike by the individual himself and those around him, until unexpectedly some incident serves to reveal the sentiment in its true intensity.

While I, personally, cannot recall being brutal at any time either intentionally or otherwise, it was not until the age of seventeen that I found that the fact of suffering awakened within me a reserve of emotional force hitherto undreamed of.

It happened one day while out walking with friends over the countryside. Unexpectedly, we came across some carters attempting to transport an impossible load of timber from the spinnery in the hollow over a steep field to the roadway above.

The team of horses worked with the agonized frenzy of slaves long accustomed to the terror of a merciless whip. But in spite of all their efforts the load was sticking, and the lead horse, who was a younger animal than the others, was inclined to disregard somewhat the rough shouts and stinging lash which urged him to greater exertions.

The carters determined that they would show the lead horse who was master, that they would teach him a lesson. They undid the harness and, leading him a little way from the team, beat him round in circles with the whip, ever widening circles; impassioned, vindictive hitting, spite, anger, bloodlust, loosed upon a fellow-worker who had done what he could and could do no more.

When the carters had done their worst, they put their lead horse back in the team, and sweaty and bloody as he was, they expected him to go on working. Oh! God, was it possible that human beings could behave like that? I doubt that outside the confines of Hell itself there is anything more detestable than the man or woman who ill-treats a fellow-creature.

To my eternal shame I cannot remember that I actually did anything, but I have been trying ever since to take the part of abused and tortured creatures. I cannot remember if the load was finally abandoned at the foot of the hill, neither can I remember if these men were brought to justice for their behaviour. I have recollection only of intense emotion created within me by the scene and of its lasting effect on my outlook on life.

Lack of understanding and ignorance are often as much the cause of suffering as is wanton cruelty. I once found a sheep-dog at a farmstead left all day in a filthy stone kennel or shed with nothing in this world to do with himself but scratch his fleas. On enquiring about him, I learnt that since he was long past work, they simply left him in his kennel. Indeed, they did not even bother to let him out to lie about a little in the sunshine. They were ignorant of their first duty to an old and well-tried servant.

I must also say something about Laddie, a young Labrador about ten months old, who exists chained in the backyard of one of the houses in the village where I am now staying.

The dog's mistress keeps a small shop. She already has more to attend to than she can manage— an elderly husband and family to look after, a shop to serve—so that even if she wished to find time for her dog, there would scarcely be opportunity for her to exercise him. I have repeatedly asked this woman why, under the circumstances, she need keep a dog at all. She replies that she has had dogs all her life, and that if Laddie is on the chain all day, it is no concern of mine.

A friend came with me to the shop the other day, and we insisted, with all the force that we could bring to bear upon the subject, on the absolute necessity of a " running chain," as being the irreducible minimum which she could do in the interests of her wretched captive. The woman retorted by saying that our interest in her affairs was a " scandalization of characters," and forthwith rang up the police to have us ejected !

Nevertheless, possibly because she was really afraïd of scandal, that running chain has gone up in her backyard, and so we have done some good in making things better for Laddie.

I naturally sympathise very deeply with all creatures kept in captivity. Some time ago a lady told me that she had once been given a pair of bull-finches which had been caught in a trap.

She caged them for some time, but when the Spring came, they almost begged to be set free, so she took them, far out into the country, and set them free in a wood.

They flew up into a tree, and sang her their thanks.

And the next winter, when the weather was especially severe, back they came to that kind lady's window for crumbs!

But they wouldn't come inside! They seemed to say " No more cage for me, thank you ! "

There is the real cruelty of the cage, but one has to face up to the fact that a bird which has been born and bred in captivity is not fit or able to fight the battles of life if suddenly freed. Canaries, for instance, might die of exposure, or be killed by other birds.

Some people, however, who keep canaries make a point of making life as happy for them as they can. I know a man and wife in Edinburgh whose flat is below the level of the street, but whose canaries are happier surely than many who are owned by less considerate people, even though their houses may be more fortunately situated. Every day these canaries are allowed to fly about the front room at will, and there are all sorts of attractive perches and swings for them *outside* the cage. Canaries need exercise just as a dog needs his daily walk.

\* \* \* \* \* \*

If a man or woman practises being kind to animals to the nth. degree, he or she may become known as a "humanitarian." Actually, everyone should be a humanitarian. The dictionary defines the word "humanity" as "the nature of man," and "kind disposition." Now if these terms were synonymous, that is to say if the nature of man had always a kind disposition, we should be very much nearer achieving progress in our civilization.

It is not given to mortal man to know the delights of a future Paradise, but because Heaven is to be found in every kind word and kindly action, there cannot be a better preparation for such a State, than the building, as far as is possible, of a Heaven on Earth.

Nearly all of us, at some time or other, have wondered what it would be like if it were a perfect world—a world without lust, oppression and cruelty. I feel that I may, therefore, be excused in quoting from H. G. Wells in *A Modern Utopia* : "In all the round world of Utopia there is no meat. There used to be. But now we cannot stand the thought of slaughter-houses. And, in a population that is all educated, and at about the same level of physical refinement, it is practically impossible to find anyone who will hew a dead ox or pig. We never settled the hygienic aspect of meat-eating at all. This other aspect decided us. I can still remember as a boy the rejoicings over the closing of the last slaughter-house."

It will be seen from the foregoing how very far removed is the world from a state of Utopia. Animals are, indeed, subject to every kind of victimization at the hand of man, yet there are to be found an abundance of men and women so educated as to concern themselves but little with the sufferings of creatures whom they may regard as instruments for their profit or pleasure.

The human animal is very divided in his opinions on other animals. Some look upon them as conveniences, while others know that their fellow-mortals have not only feelings but rights. Undoubtedly, however, a tremendous amount of good could be effected in the interests of every creature if animal lovers would bestir themselves. There are many among us who have fallen under the spell of S. Francis of Assisi, and who regard cruelty to animals, in whatever guise it may appear, as a crime which incites a challenge.

## A PASS TO CLIMB.

WHEN the cares of this world are heavy, one of the best ways to shoulder the load is to put a pack upon your back, and go out on tramp. It is hardly possible that any active person should not benefit by becoming a vagabond even for a single night.

It is a night in early September, a night of stars, and the moon is up. I have joined a party of ramblers who know the heather paths of the Trossachs as do the mountain sheep. My companions carry tents in their rucksacks, and we are footing it up the Duke's Pass—the highway which connects Aberfoyle and Loch Katrine. Soon, however, we shall leave the roadway, and strike off across the moors for Brig o' Turk.

September is known to the old Gaels as the month of peace. Our camping ground is six or seven miles ahead, but a gentle breeze serves to refresh us as we press onwards.

One of the lads is a disciple of Burns, and as he walks he sings, and his voice does not obtrude itself on the calm of the sweet evening.

> " Of a' the airts the wind can blaw
> I dearly lo'e the west,
> For there the bonnie lassie lives,
> The lassie I lo'e best ;
> Let wild woods grow and rivers flow,
> Wi' mony a hill between,
> Baith day and night my fancy's flight,
> Is ever wi' my Jean."

No road is ever too long if one had a grand old song like that in one's heart. Every true vagabond should have a song on his lips, save when he is reserving his energy for strenuous climbing. And the call of the open road has in itself been the theme of some of our most perfect songs ; for is not the message of hope expressed in the upward sweep of the roadway, is there not joy in the moon and stars which light the way, and romance in the roadside fire ?

Now the night is already well advanced, and lately the leader of the party has been setting a good pace. I, for one, am terribly thirsty. Fortunately, after some time we come across a spring which gushes over the hillside, and each of us in turn stoops to drink from it. Wine in a crystal goblet or beer in a pewter tankard would compare but poorly with this water from the hillside spring.

We rest a little, and then go forward again. All around us are the most glorious solitudes. On our right we pass Loch Drunkie, a jewel embedded in the heather hills, and so at length we have come to the rough post which indicates the path which we may follow to Brig o' Turk.

Once on the moor we proceed in single file. Here some caution is necessary since the consequences of a twisted ankle so far from home would be serious indeed. Nevertheless, the last few miles are easy down the glen.

The camping ground we have chosen is a stretch of meadow adjoining the Creag Dhu Hostel of the Scottish Youth Hostels Association.

When the tents are pitched, I go alone to the water's edge of Loch Achray not far distant. The gypsies are at their evening camp fire, and the moon sends a golden road of light over the loch.

Were they not scenes such as this which inspired Liszt in the writing of the Hungarian Rhapsodies? I am thinking of one of the Rhapsodies, now, it is the second in D. minor and G., to which many may have listened without perhaps fully appreciating the emotions underlying it.

In the boyhood of Liszt, wandering gypsies used to camp near the village in which he lived, so that he had an opportunity of studying them and their music. And for myself at least the wild and varying rhythms which characterise the Hungarian Rhapsodies, will ever express the freedom of the out-of-doors, the night wanderings of a nomad, and the ecstatic delight of communion with the things of nature.

This is the temple of Peace. Here, by the moonlit loch, one can for a while cease to strive for mastery in those things which the hand of Time will destroy.

Moreover, I find a great lesson of humility in the poignant beauty of calm at nightfall. S. Paul reminds us in one of the Epistles that *one star differeth from another in glory*. Yet there are many who hope to set themselves up above their neighbours, and there are those who cannot meet members of other nations as brothers, because they think that they are superior to them. People are still arguing as to who shall be the greatest, and perhaps they always will.

But my footsteps and my thoughts have carried me too far.

I must return to camp ground.

One need take with one but the simplest requirements to make a tramp holiday a complete success, for there is equal enjoyment alike for rich and poor among those who are wise enough to go tramping in beautiful country. My four tramp mates, however, carry with them a musical instrument apiece, the one has a ukulele, another a mouth-organ, another a penny whistle, and another a Jew's harp.

Therefore, after we have consumed a simple meal of bread, scones and fruit, the four fellows strike up a band ; and although, musically, its performance might be regarded as being outside serious consideration, yet it is very good fun, and that is the main thing.

Our tents are pitched to overlook the Loch, behind which towers Ben Venue, which is a noble summit akin to Ben Ledi and Ben Lomond.

In the morning we shall take the road back, each to his several duties in the haunts of men. We may go either to the hewing of stone or the drawing of water, but for the time being we ask only this comradeship which joys in simple things.

For myself there can be no end to this journey, so long as I have strength to pursue the roadway which leads on I know not whither. Yet it is possible for me to look back and see where I went wrong, and thus I learn to find my way more rightly in the future.

All our lives are a journey, but I am convinced, by listening to the experiences of others, that the happiest among us are those who go about making life more happy for their fellow-mortals, human and non-human.

I lie in my tent and wait for sleep, and above through the open doors, I may take delight in " the splendid joy of the stars."